Stratford Library Association
2203 Main Street
Stratford, CT 06615
203-385-4160

W9-BRW-857

Native Americans

The Algonquin

Richard M. Gaines

ABDO Publishing Company

visit us at
www.abdopub.com

Published by ABDO Publishing Company, 4940 Viking Drive, Suite 622, Edina, Minnesota 55435. Copyright © 2000 Abdo Consulting Group, Inc., Pentagon Tower, P.O. Box 36036, Minneapolis, Minnesota 55435 USA. International copyrights reserved in all countries. No part of this book may be reproduced in any form without written permission from the publisher.

Published 2000
Printed in the United States of America
Second printing 2002

Illustrator: David Fadden (pgs. 7, 9, 11, 13, 15, 17, 19, 21, 23, 25, 27)
Cover Photo: Corbis
Interior Photos: Corbis (pgs. 4, 24); The Anishinabe Experience (pgs. 29, 30)
Editors: Bob Italia, Tamara L. Britton, Kate A. Furlong
Art Direction & Maps: Pat Laurel

Library of Congress Cataloging-in-Publication Data

Gaines, Richard, 1942-
    The Algonquin / Richard M. Gaines.
        p. cm. -- (Native Americans)
    Includes bibliographical references and index.
    Summary: Presents a brief introduction to the Algonquin Indians, including information on their homes, society, food, clothing, family life, and life today.
    ISBN 1-57765-383-1
    1. Algonquin Indians--Juvenile literature. [1. Algonquin Indians. 2. Indians of North America.] I. Title.

E99.A349 G35 2000
971.3004'973--dc21

                                                                        00-023767

Special thanks to Contributing Editor
BOB GOULAIS, COMMUNICATIONS OFFICER
Anishinabek Nation
and to
Linda Sarazin of the Anishinabe Experience

Illustrator: David Kanietakeron Fadden

David Kanietakeron Fadden is a member of the Akwesasne Mohawk Wolf Clan. His work has appeared in publications such as *Akwesasne Notes, Indian Time,* and the *Northeast Indian Quarterly.* Examples of his work have also appeared in various publications of the Six Nations Indian Museum in Onchiota, NY. His work has also appeared in "How The West Was Lost: Always The Enemy," produced by Gannett Production which appeared on the Discovery Channel. David's work has been exhibited in Albany, NY; the Lake Placid Center for the Arts; Centre Strathearn in Montreal, Quebec; North Country Community College in Saranac Lake, NY; Paul Smiths College in Paul Smiths, NY; and at the Unison Arts & Learning Center in New Paltz, NY.

Contents

Where They Lived

The Algonquin (AL-GON-KWIN) are members of the Anishinabek (A-NISH-NAW-BEK) Nation. People of the Anishinabek Nation live in the eastern woodlands on both sides of the Great Lakes. The Anishinabek people include the Algonquin, Ojibwa or Chippewa, Delaware, Mississauga, Odawa, and Potawatami.

Some historians believe the Algonquin came from Asia to North America about 6,000 years ago. Others think the Algonquin have

The northern woods of Ontario, Canada

been in North America much longer. Anishinabek **elders** teach that the Algonquin have lived in North America since time began.

The Algonquin settled along the St. Lawrence River south of the St. Maurice River and west along the Ottawa River. Part of the Algonquin lands are called the northern woods. The northern woods is a land of rocks and shallow soil. It is covered with birch and many kinds of evergreen trees. Everywhere, there are pure lakes and rivers.

The Algonquin speak **Algonquian** (AL-GON-KWEE-ANN). But, not all Algonquian-speaking peoples are Algonquin. Other Native American nations and tribes speak Algonquian, including the Cheyenne, Arapaho, Blackfoot, and Cree.

The Algonquin people settled in the present-day Canadian provinces of Quebec and Ontario.

Society

In the 1600s, the Algonquin people split into eight or ten large **bands**. Several men led these bands, including the chief and **medicine man**. During the summer, the bands camped together.

In the winter, the bands divided into much smaller groups. Often, just one or two family **clans** made a small winter camp in their hunting grounds. Men of the family directed the clans.

The Algonquin were not farmers. The summer was too short to grow crops. Instead, they lived by hunting, fishing, and gathering. So, **preserving** the family hunting grounds was important. Sons **inherited** the right to hunt and fish there.

An Algonquin camp in winter and summer

Homes

All Anishinabek lived in different types of wigwam (WIG-WAM). The word *wigwam* means "home."

According to Anishinabek teachings, men were responsible for building the wigwam. Wigwams were made by placing thin tree branches or **saplings** in the ground in a circle. They were tied together at the top to make either a dome or a cone. A hole was left at the top. It let out the smoke from the fire inside.

To make the outside of the wigwam, women sewed strips of birch bark or animal hides to thin branches. They placed each section around the wigwam frame from the bottom upwards. Each section overlapped the others.

In the winter, the Anishinabek covered the wigwam floor with spruce branches. The branches were covered with animal skins to make a warm floor. When the Anishinabek wanted to move, they took the outside coverings and floor coverings with them. They left the wigwam frame behind.

Wigwam construction: 1. Building the frame
2. Attaching the birch bark sections 3. A finished wigwam

Food

According to Anishinabek teachings, the "kwe-wuk" (KWAY-WUK) women were responsible for gathering wild rice, berries, and maple syrup. Sometimes, the women and children planted crops such as corn, beans, and squash. The women also did some animal trapping.

The "nini" (NIH-NIH) men hunted moose, caribou, deer, porcupine, beaver, and bear in their family hunting grounds.

In the winter, hunters wearing snowshoes followed moose tracks. The moose were easily caught because their thin legs got stuck in the deep snow.

The Algonquin fished in many different ways. At night, they put a bright torch in the **bow** of a canoe. Then, they speared the fish that were attracted to the light. In the winter, they cut holes in the lake ice. Then, they fished with hooks and spears.

The Algonquin also used large, complex traps called "fish fences" to catch their fish. Non-native commercial **anglers** still use these traps today.

An Algonquin woman gathering wild rice

Clothing

The Algonquin wore deerskin **tunics**. Women's tunics were longer than men's, ending below the knees. The men wore **breechcloths** and tight leggings. Everyone wore moccasins.

In the winter, the Algonquin wore large robes made of animal skins. They used the robes as sleeping bags. They also wore mittens, hoods, and fur caps.

In the spring, the Algonquin wore sleeveless tunics. And they did not wear leggings. They often smeared their bodies with animal grease. This protected their exposed skin from mosquitoes.

Traditional dress in winter (left) and summer

Crafts

In June and July, birch tree bark could be easily peeled off the tree in large, unbroken sheets. Then, the bark was separated into paper-thin sheets.

The Algonquin used birch bark for many things. They made cups by folding the bark into a cone shape and fastening it with sticks. They made boxes and dishes the same way. Boxes, dishes, and cups were often decorated with porcupine quills. The quills were colored with natural dyes.

Large rolls of birch bark were used to make cradles. The bottom of the cradles were lined with moss. Even the wigwams were covered with birch bark.

The most amazing use of birch bark was to build canoes. Birch-bark canoes were strong but light. Two men could carry a 25-foot (7.6-m) canoe 4 miles (6.4 km) without resting. The canoe could hold 3,000 pounds (1,361 kg) of **cargo** and 10 people.

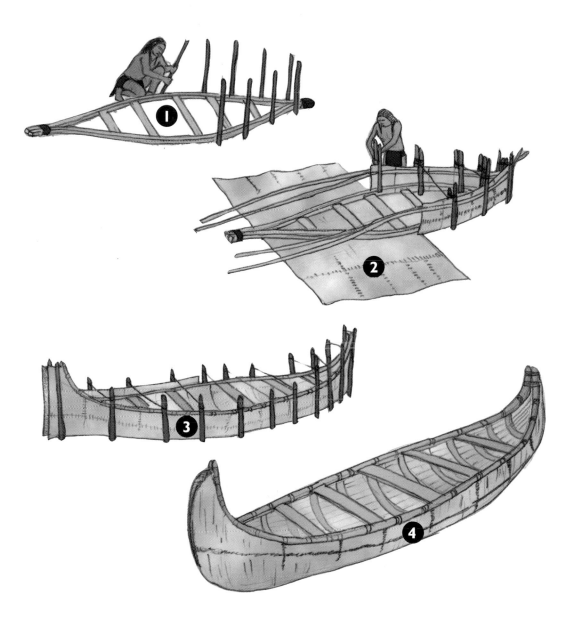

Building a birch-bark canoe: 1. A frame forms the outline of the canoe. 2. Bark is folded up around the frame. 3. Seams are sealed with resin and bent cedar ribs are installed on the inside. 4. A finished birch-bark canoe.

Family

All Algonquin were members of a **clan**. Each clan was named after an animal, such as the turtle or the loon. The animal watched over and protected the entire family.

In the clan system, the oldest man was the leader or chief. He decided how best to use the family hunting grounds. Algonquin families were careful not to over-hunt. The teachings say to always think and plan for the Seventh **Generation**.

Algonquin people did not believe in land ownership. Instead, they believed the Creator and Mother Earth gave them the land in trust. It was important that the land, water, air, animals, and plants were cared for.

Chiefs and important spiritual leaders settled disputes in pow-wows, or gatherings. During these gatherings, the leaders smoked the **sacred** pipe to bring about the Seven Grandfather Teachings. They are the Anishinabek's most important teachings. The Seven Grandfather Teachings are Love, Honesty, Truth, Respect, Bravery, Humility, and Wisdom.

The entire Anishinabek Nation gathered many times in its history. These gatherings brought together the Three Fires **Confederacy**. It was a group of peoples whose languages and lands were close. They met together for military and political purposes.

When family members died, they were buried in their best clothes. Favorite objects were placed in graves that were lined with bark and covered with earth. Grieving family members placed **tobacco** in the grave.

Algonquin leaders smoking a sacred pipe

Children

Each **clan** member had an animal friend. When a child was born, everyone in the family, especially the mother, waited for the first animal to appear at the wigwam. Sometimes, it took a year or more. When the animal appeared, it was never disturbed. It was allowed to view the baby and leave.

Often, the child was named after the animal. The child learned to be friends with this animal all his or her life. This animal was called the child's *wisana*.

When the child was old enough to walk, he or she helped the mother gather wood, water, and food. Girls continued to help their mothers throughout their entire lives. Boys learned to hunt and fight.

Next page:
An Algonquin girl picks berries while two boys practice their hunting skills.

Myths

The Algonquin believed in a supreme being, known as the G'zheminidoo (SZHEM-IN-UH-DOW) or Great Spirit. The Great Spirit was worshipped as the Creator of everything.

The Algonquin also believed in a **supernatural** half-man/half-spirit named Waynaboozhoo. Waynaboozhoo was also called "Original Man." When Anishinabek people greet each other, they say "boozhoo." It is a word that pays respect to the Original Man.

Some children's stories also tell of Waynaboozhoo's life. He teased and played tricks on the spirits and people he met in the forest.

The Algonquin loved Waynaboozhoo. But, they feared the Windigo. The Windigo was a bad spirit. He ate anyone he met in the dark and lonely parts of the forest.

The spirit called "Mushkoday-nini" (MUSH-KOW-DAY-NIH-NIH) is a lost brother of Waynaboozhoo. He lives in the dense woods.

The Algonquin also believed in a tribe of powerful, Little People. They, too, lived in the forest. The Algonquin also believe in the Sasquatch. It is also known as bigfoot.

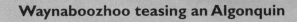

Waynaboozhoo teasing an Algonquin

War

The Algonquin based their relationships with other Native Americans and Europeans on trust and friendship. The only wars resulted from attempts to control the fur trade. In the 1500s, some Algonquin bands became enemies of the Iroquois. Each wanted to control the fur trade with the French.

In the 1620s, the Algonquin became enemies of their old allies, the Huron and the French. The Algonquin were soon forced to abandon their hunting lands along the St. Lawrence River.

Tribal warfare was cruel. Attackers would kill all of the men. The women and children were forced to live in the attacker's camps.

Algonquin warriors used a long bow and arrows, knives, hatchets, or war clubs in surprise raids along forest trails or in enemy camps. They also used wooden shields to protect themselves.

Sometimes, **raids** were made hundreds of miles into enemy territory. Being able to travel unseen and unheard was an important skill of Algonquin warriors.

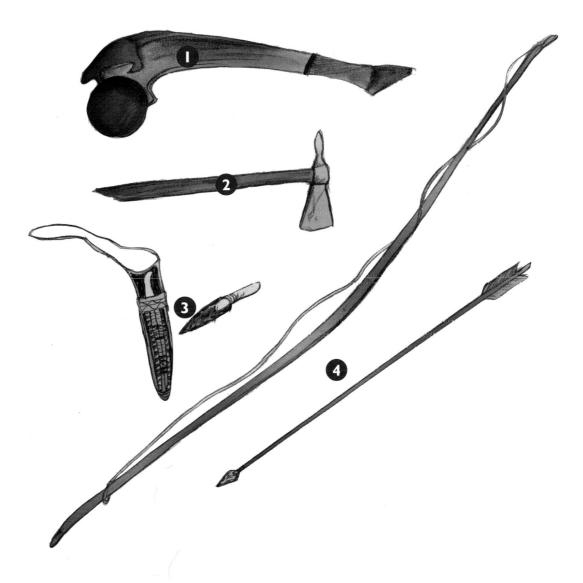

Algonquin weapons: 1. War club 2. Hatchet 3. Knife with sheath 4. Bow and arrow

Contact with Europeans

Samuel de Champlain

In 1603, French explorer Samuel de Champlain met an Algonquin war party in the Ottawa River valley. The Algonquin warriors were returning from a successful battle with the Iroquois.

Champlain later met with other Anishinabek people including the Ojibwa or Chippewa, Odawa, and Nipissing people. These Native Americans made trade treaties with the French and the Dutch. They traded furs for European guns, cloth, and axes.

During the 1800s, European settlers spread many diseases to the Algonquin. The Algonquin had no natural defenses against these diseases. Many Algonquin died. The tribe never regained its power.

The Anishinabek people entered into many treaties with the British, French, and colonial governments. These treaties were agreements between two nations. In them, the Anishinabek agreed to share the land and natural resources with the European settlers.

Gradually, the Algonquin were forced from their homes along the St. Lawrence River. They settled along rivers that flowed into the Ottawa River. Around 1870, the Algonquin received several small **reservations** from the Canadian government.

Trading furs for cloth

Iroquet

Iroquet was an Algonquin chief. He first met Samuel de Champlain in June 1609, near Quebec. The Algonquin and their Huron neighbors made an alliance with the French to make war on the Iroquois.

The next year, Iroquet agreed to take a young French boy to his home. He taught him the Algonquin ways and language. Champlain agreed to take a young Algonquin boy to France with him. This arrangement worked well. The next year, two French boys spent the winter with Iroquet in his home.

Relations between the French and the Algonquin continued to improve. In 1615, Champlain and some of his soldiers visited the Algonquin homelands. Iroquet continued to lead his tribe for many years.

The Algonquin Today

Today, the Algonquin are known as the Algonquin Nation. It is a member of the greater Anishinabek Nation. It is made up of 43 First Nations across Ontario, Canada. The Anishinabek Nation has a Grand Council Chief. He speaks for all Anishinabek people.

About 4,000 Algonquin live in ten communities scattered in Ontario and Quebec. Many more Algonquin are spread across Canada and the United States. They live on small plots of land as hunters, trappers, and guides.

Many Algonquin have married other Native Americans, especially the Cree and Ojibwa. They have also married whites and have moved to nearby towns.

Today, the Algonquin are beginning to reunite. Many live in what is now known as Algonquins of Pikwàkanagàn First Nation. It has about 2. 8 square miles (7.2 sq k) of land on Golden Lake, near Pembroke, Ontario. It is governed by a chief and **council**. More than 1,700 people live there. Most Algonquins live off the **reservation** because there are not many jobs there.

Most Algonquin children attend Canadian schools. The **traditional** ways of teaching were becoming lost because of the residential schools.

Tanning hides at Pikwàkanagàn

In the early 1900s, children were removed from their homes and families. They were sent far away to residential schools. Algonquin children were forced to cut their long hair. They were forbidden to speak their Anishinabek language.

Today, many Algonquin **elders** cannot speak their language because of their experiences at residential schools. But now, Algonquin children are beginning to learn more about their **culture** and language. In school, children can re-learn their Algonquin language. It is now part of their classroom studies.

Algonquin children and adults take part in their culture. Some boys learn the skill of fishing and trapping from their fathers and grandfathers. Some girls learn the responsibilities of the Anishinabek kwe-wuk.

The most exciting family activity is the modern-day pow-wow. It is no longer just for chiefs and spiritual leaders. It is a celebration of culture, song, dance, and a gathering of new and old friends.

The men sing around the big drum, called the Grandfather Drum. They sing songs about friendship, travel, hunting, and love. Sometimes, many drums take part in a pow-wow. Both men and women wear fancy clothing. They dance clockwise around the Grandfather Drums in the arbour (drum pit).

There are three main types of male dancers. The male **Traditional** Dancer wears mostly buckskin. A large feather is bustled on the small of his back. The Traditional Dancer dances with slow, powerful steps.

An Algonquin Fancy Dancer

The Fancy Dancer wears colorful clothing. He has two colorful feather bustles on his back. He dances fast and with lots of energy.

The Grass Dancer came from the western tribes. Colorful strands of yarn or ribbon are draped down his clothing. He dances as though he is swaying like long sweetgrass.

There are also three main types of female dancers. The female Traditional Dancer wears a long buckskin dress with fancy beads.

The Shawl Dancer dresses and dances like the male Fancy Dancer. But instead of the feather bustles, she wears a shawl around her back.

The final type of female dancer is very special. The Jingle Dress Dancer wears a cotton dress made of hoofs or tin cones. When the "jingles" ring together, they make a sacred sound. The Jingle Dress first appeared in the Anishinabek Nation. It is used mostly for healing.

Glossary

Algonquian - the group of tribes that speak related Algonquian languages.

angler - a person who fishes.

band - a number of persons acting together; a subgroup of a tribe.

bow - the front part of a ship or boat.

breechcloth - a soft piece of hide or cloth, usually worn by men, that was wrapped between the legs and tied with a belt. It was worn instead of pants.

cargo - a load of goods.

clan - all the people in a single tribe who claim to be descended from the same first ancestor. Some tribes had clans that were passed on to the children by the mother's family and some by the father's family.

confederacy - a group of people joined together for a special purpose.

council - a group of people called together to give advice and to discuss or settle questions.

culture - the customs, arts, and tools of a nation or people at a certain time.

elder - a person having authority because of age or experience.

generation - the people born in the same period.

inherit - to receive from one's parents or ancestors.

medicine man - a spiritual leader of a tribe or nation.

preserve - to keep from harm or change.

raid - a sudden attack.

reservation - land set aside by a treaty with the government for the home of a Native American tribe.

resin - a sticky substance that flows from some trees.

sacred - holy.

sapling - a thin, young tree.

supernatural - above or beyond the forces or laws of nature.

tobacco - a medicine plant used in ceremonies.

tradition - the handing down of beliefs, customs, and stories from parents to children.

tunic - a short, close-fitting garment.

Web Sites

The official Web site of the Anishinabek Nation: **http://www.anishinabek.ca/**

The Anishinabe Experience (**http://www.anishexp.com/index.html**) invites you to enter the world of the Algonquin of Pikwàkanagàn (Golden Lake, Ontario, Canada). Learn how they maintain their culture, traditions, and beliefs.

These sites are subject to change. Go to your favorite search engine and type in "Algonquin" for more sites.

Index